CRAPPY
to
Happy

SIMPLE STEPS *to live your*
BEST LIFE

CRAPPY *to* Happy

CASSANDRA DUNN

Hardie Grant
BOOKS

Cassandra Dunn is a clinical and coaching psychologist and an experienced mindfulness educator, workshop facilitator and keynote speaker. Cass is the expert psychologist for trainer Tiffiny Hall's online health and fitness program, tiffxo.com, and she regularly shares her insights on happiness, mindfulness and wellbeing in print and digital media. She also hosts the wildly popular *Crappy to Happy* podcast, which has reached over 2 million downloads. Cass lives on the Sunshine Coast in Queensland with her husband, daughter and a menagerie of rescued animals.

Connect with Cass online

facebook: **cassandradunn.psychologist**

instagram/twitter: **cassdunn_xo**

cassandradunn.com.au

For Annabelle
who brings ultimate joy and
meaning to my life every day

CONTENTS

CONTENTS

INTRODUCTION

Have you ever had the thought, 'I'll be happy when ...'?

Perhaps for you happiness will arrive in the form of a pay rise or a new job, a holiday, a marriage (or divorce), an updated kitchen or that divine pair of shoes you've had your eye on. Consciously or not, most of us are hankering for something. Whether happiness is somewhere on the distant horizon or just around the corner, it rarely feels like we are holding it in our hands. As humans, we are driven to achieve and evolve. Working towards goals gives us meaning and purpose, but somewhere along the way we seem to have forgotten that happiness is already within reach, if we could just slow down enough to see it.

The cliché is true: happiness truly is in the journey, not the destination.

For many years, before training as a clinical psychologist, I worked as a life coach, helping people achieve their goals. It was immensely satisfying to assist people to gain the tools and skills they needed to move from being stuck and lacking clarity or direction to gaining momentum and achieving success. People set goals in all areas of life – money, weight loss, relationships, career. I helped them find the courage to make changes and to clarify the actions necessary to achieve these goals.

Coaching, by definition, aims to help people who are already psychologically healthy and functioning well to aim even higher: to flourish, thrive and achieve optimum success and satisfaction. During those years, I heard many success coaches and motivational speakers give inspired seminars on how we could raise our bars higher, get out of our own way and achieve smashing success. I saw many success stories, but I also saw many people walk away from those events full of optimism and renewed vigour, only to have their motivation wane as soon as they returned to the real world, where they had to deal with their old self-doubts and fears. They wound up feeling even more deflated and disappointed, often blaming themselves for their lack of persistent action.

I do believe that success and happiness are available to all of us. I do not believe that happiness is found in fame, fortune, a 'bikini body', a seven-figure income or a holiday house on the beach. Those things are nice to have, but real happiness is found in a sense of purpose and meaning in life, in mutually supportive relationships, in self-acceptance and contributing to the greater good. It's in dropping the endless pursuit of 'personal development' and giving yourself some love right now. It's taking some time to be still and giving your busy brain a break from all the thinking, worrying, and striving to be better.

Most importantly, happiness can be found right here and now, not in some picture-perfect ideal life. Goal striving is certainly associated with higher levels of wellbeing, but when the ceaseless pursuit of goals shifts your focus away from the things that can be appreciated right now, it's counterproductive to your health and happiness.

As a clinical and coaching psychologist and mindfulness meditation teacher, I work with people across the full spectrum of psychological mood and functioning – from those with a diagnosable mental illness such as depression or anxiety through to the reasonably well but 'languishing', and even those who would describe themselves as very happy and successful, but who want to cultivate a deeper sense of wellbeing.

I have come to believe that most people, no matter where they are along that spectrum, can benefit from information and strategies that will support them to be more happy, more of the time. It's currently estimated that less than 20 per cent of adults are truly flourishing in life. I think that number could easily increase if people

> "Most people, no matter where they are along that spectrum, can benefit from information and strategies that will support them to be more happy, more of the time."

were equipped with the tools and know-how. I especially believe that even though most people will never set foot in a psychologist's office (and probably don't need to), this shouldn't preclude them from having access to the kind of information and tools that we psychologists know will enhance the quality of their lives.

I'm especially interested in helping women feel less crappy and more happy, because I know from my own experience, and from working with thousands of others, that most women will put themselves last every time, forgoing their own happiness for the sake of others'. Women especially are overwhelmed by busyness, crippled by perfectionism, and plagued by a sense of inadequacy, hate for their bodies, and guilt about pretty much everything. It doesn't have to be this way.

In 2015 I launched a free seven-day email course called 'Crappy to Happy'. Over 1000 people subscribed within the first month. Similarly, when I created the *Crappy to Happy* podcast with my good friend and fitness trainer Tiffiny Hall in 2017, it was downloaded over 1.5 million times in less than a year. It now averages 150,000 downloads per month. People are starving for simple, practical tips to help them live a more fulfilling and satisfying life.

I would love for the *Crappy to Happy* book to continue expanding on the conversation, providing more information and tools to help you live your best life. Everyone deserves to feel less crappy and more happy, and I hope this book will give you the simple, straightforward and practical advice you need to help you to achieve just that!

Step one

CHOOSE
HAPPINESS

A huge range of good feelings fall under the broad umbrella of what we generally call 'happiness'.

To feel happy is to feel joyful or content or buoyant or grateful, or any of a long list of sweet, positive emotions. Not only is it a pleasant feeling, but the attainment of happiness is often touted as the whole point of living. Greek philosopher Aristotle (384–322 BCE) said, 'Happiness is the meaning and the purpose of life, the whole aim and end of human existence.' He might have been on to something. Even now, thousands of years later, people frequently cite 'being happy' as the ultimate goal. What do all parents want for their children? 'It doesn't matter what they do or achieve,' we say, 'just as long as they're happy.'

It seems so simple, but a clear definition of happiness is a little harder to pin down. If happiness is the experience of positive emotions, is it therefore the absence of negative emotions? That seems unrealistic. Perhaps it would be fairer to say it's having more positive emotions than negative. Is it in fact more than a passing feeling (even though we experience it as a feeling), and actually a state of being that involves being fully engaged with life or having a deep sense of purpose? Is it to be free of adversity and struggle? Given that this is a book about happiness, it seems important that we clear this up. That way, as you move through the concepts and strategies I'm sharing with you, we're on the same page when it comes to what it really means to be happy.

In psychology, some terms used to describe and measure what we might generally call 'happiness' include 'subjective wellbeing' or 'satisfaction with life'. These descriptors refer to your subjective experience of feeling pleasure or contentment.

There is, however, a more stable and enduring definition of happiness.

Happiness isn't just
about feeling good.

Happiness is also the satisfaction that comes from knowing your life has meaning and purpose.

For this reason, Professor Martin Seligman, known as the father of Positive Psychology, made the decision to drop the word 'happiness' and replace it with 'wellbeing'. Achieving optimal wellbeing is now commonly referred to as 'flourishing', and this describes much more than simply experiencing a pleasant mood. For the purposes of this book, I am using the word 'happiness' interchangeably with terms such as 'wellbeing', 'flourishing' and 'thriving', but it will become clear throughout the steps ahead that there's more to real, sustainable happiness than simply feeling cheerful all the time.

The experience of pleasant emotions is sometimes referred to as hedonic wellbeing, from the Greek *hēdonē*, meaning pleasure. This is the way you feel when you laugh with friends, enjoy a delicious meal, slide into bed between crisp clean sheets or soak your tired body in a warm bath. It might be the excited buzz of booking a holiday or finally renovating your tired old kitchen. Hedonic happiness refers to those warm feelings that are derived from sensory pleasures or material gains.

Hedonic wellbeing
(Greek *hēdonē*) pleasure

Eudaemonic wellbeing
(Greek *eu̱dai̱monía*)
self-realisation and
fulfilment of potential

Eudaemonic wellbeing, on the other hand, derives from the Greek *eudaimonía* and refers to a version of happiness that is achieved by self-realisation and the fulfilment of your potential in life. This kind of happiness is associated with your engagement with life and your sense of purpose. Doing meaningful work, striving to reach your potential, or, as Maslow called it, 'self-actualisation', and committing to causes beyond your own self-interest all fall into the broad category of eudaemonic wellbeing. These things don't always feel pleasant. In fact, some of the experiences that evoke the most uncomfortable and even painful emotions,

"Some of the experiences that evoke the most uncomfortable and even painful emotions are the experiences that also give us the greatest sense of meaning and therefore, paradoxically, the greatest joy."

such as parenting, having tough conversations, or sitting with others through their illness or heartbreak, are the experiences that also give us the greatest sense of meaning and therefore, paradoxically, the greatest joy.

I believe that a complete definition of happiness needs to incorporate both of these aspects of wellbeing. Psychologist and leading happiness researcher Sonja Lyubomirsky, in her 2007 book *The How of Happiness*, defines happiness as 'the experience of joy, contentment, or positive well-being, combined with a sense that one's life is good, meaningful, and worthwhile'.

FROM ANCIENT WISDOM TO MODERN SCIENCE

2600 years ago Siddhartha Guatama was a young prince living near the border of Nepal and India, being raised in an environment designed purely for his pleasure. His father, the king, made sure the young prince had everything he could possibly wish for, and was determined that he would never witness suffering, illness, ageing or death. The story goes that at the age of twenty-nine, during an outing beyond the palace walls, the prince was accidentally exposed to the truth about life's adversity and the inevitability of illness and death. That was when he realised real happiness would never come from his external world; that it must come from within his own mind. He fled the confines of his castle, leaving behind his new wife and young child, to become a spiritual seeker. In stark contrast to his privileged upbringing, he joined a band of ascetics who sought enlightenment by denying themselves all creature comforts and worldly pleasures, sometimes consuming only one grain of rice in a day. He realised that this was not the way to be free of mental suffering either.

After six years, determined to reach an enlightened state of mind, he sat under a Bodhi tree for four days and nights until he broke through his mental barriers and realised the truth of happiness. He became known as the Buddha, and spent the next forty-five years teaching what he'd learned. One of his teachings refers to 'The Middle Path', which is the balance between a life that is focused only on self-interest or personal gain and a life that is focused only on sacrifice and contribution. When I think about the balance of pleasure and purpose in achieving happiness, I'm often reminded of the Buddha's 'Middle Path' approach to life. This, together with many of his other lessons about mindfulness and acceptance, has become embedded within current approaches to Western psychological practice. Buddha's teachings have proven to be reliable and valid tools for reducing suffering and increasing psychological and emotional wellbeing. This isn't a book about Buddhism, but the relevance of those philosophies and their application to modern psychology can't be ignored.

Happiness is a choice

Years of research into human emotions and wellbeing have proven that we all have the power to increase the amount of happiness we experience. It's true that we each have a unique biological make-up that we can't do much to change. You are born with a certain temperament – you might naturally be quite a cheerful person, or you might be more inclined to experience a lower mood, or even anxiety. Psychologists use the term 'set point' to describe your naturally occurring, base level of happiness, which they believe accounts for roughly 50 per cent of your happiness. Circumstances in your life will also affect your mood, but not as much as you might expect. In fact, some researchers argue that only 10 per cent of your happiness is attributed to external factors, such as whether you're married or single, what kind of job you have or where you live. Whether you experience great adversity or extreme good fortune, these events will often only affect your happiness for a short time before you come back to your 'set point'.

Happiness =
50% set point +
10% external factors +
40% your own choices

That leaves a full 40 per cent of your happiness in your own hands, attributable to your intentional thoughts and activities; that is, how you choose to think, where you choose to focus your physical and mental energy, how you invest your time, and the people you surround yourself with. These things are all up to you.

It's that 40 per cent that I'm interested in. I've seen countless people peg their happiness on the next goal, the next job, house, destination, pay rise or relationship when the fact is, those things count for very little in the scheme of things. And all the while, the happiness that was there for the taking went unnoticed. The strategies in this book are intended to help you incorporate more of the thoughts and behaviours into your life that will give you the best chance of maximising your 40 per cent.

Recent research has shown that our brains are able to continue growing and developing throughout the lifespan, which means some of these happiness-enhancing strategies may even raise your happiness set point permanently. This is perhaps the most exciting finding in the fields of psychology and neuroscience in recent decades. For a long time, we believed that once your brain finished developing, there was no chance of ever growing new brain cells. Now we know that isn't the case. Regardless of what has happened in your life up to this point and how your brain has been wired as a result of your genetics and/or environment, it is possible to develop new neural pathways. You can rewire your brain for more happiness in the future with the habits and choices you make today.

Why happiness matters

Research has shown that happier, more optimistic people are healthier, live longer and have more satisfying relationships than unhappy people. They perform better on the job and are more likely to be promoted. They show more resilience in the face of adversity, and they are more interested in learning, exploring and making new discoveries for the benefit of us all. They demonstrate more complex problem-solving abilities and greater capacity for innovation and lateral thinking. Happy people are more altruistic, tending to be more involved in their communities and supportive of other people's causes. Far from being selfish or superficial, the pursuit of your own happiness may in fact have far-reaching benefits for your family and your community and around the world.

Every idea and strategy presented in this book is supported by science. The information is presented in short, easily digestible steps, with each covering one main approach to happiness. My hope is that this book will prove to be a treasure chest of wisdom that you can pick up any time and quickly grasp an idea that you can immediately apply. I want to convince you that your happiness matters, and to inspire you to take action.

"Far from being selfish or superficial, the pursuit of your own happiness may in fact have far-reaching benefits for your family and your community and around the world."

CHOOSING HAPPINESS

Be curious

One of the greatest impediments to learning new ways of thinking or behaving is our tendency to have automatic thoughts such as 'I already know this', 'I've tried this before', or 'That won't work for me'. I encourage you to let go of those thoughts and try out the suggestions in this book. What works for one person won't necessarily work for another, but it is only by adopting an attitude of curiosity and open-mindedness that you will discover what works for you. I'm not asking you to take my word for anything – let your own experience be your guide.

Put happiness first

Many people focus on achieving success, believing that it will bring them happiness. In fact, the opposite is more likely to be true. Building a more positive mindset has been shown to boost your productivity, creativity and engagement, both in life and at work. It will increase your resilience and improve the quality of your relationships. All of these factors will ultimately lead to success. So rather than chasing status and achievement, pursue happiness instead, and allow success to follow.

Just notice

To make any change, you first need to notice what's happening already. Much of our daily routine (both our thoughts and our actions) is performed out of habit rather than conscious choice. Start with the intention to notice your routine thoughts and behaviours.
How often do you default to thinking patterns that negatively affect your mood? How often do you react emotionally, creating rifts in relationships or causing hurt to yourself or others? Try to notice without judgement, and use your observations as a starting point for making positive change.

Step two

BE LESS BUSY

If you've ever tried pinning someone down for dinner or planning a night out with friends, you know firsthand the problem of busyness in our modern lives.

How often have you bumped into a friend and asked, 'How are you?' only to have them reply, 'Great. Busy!' before they dash off, takeaway coffee in hand, to attend to the pressing demands of the day. I know there have been many times when I've been the one to yell 'Gotta go! Must catch up. Text me!' over my shoulder as I race off. It seems we're all *very busy*, constantly needing to be somewhere or do something.

As a society, we have collectively subscribed to the idea that a busy life is a worthwhile or meaningful one.

Being busy has almost become a competition sport. Conversations are dominated by the topic of how little free time we all have. In a world that prizes productivity and achievement, it's easy to get trapped in the cycle of 'do more, be more, have more', conflating how busy you are with how popular, important or valued you are.

At some point though, we need to face the fact that the speed at which we're hurtling through our lives allows little time to pause and reflect on whether the things we're doing are actually making us happy. We've become so consumed with all the rushing and doing that we're failing to consider the consequences of our endlessly busy lives.

> **"The speed at which we're hurtling through our lives allows little time to pause and reflect on whether the things we're doing are actually making us happy."**

A BUSY MIND

Being 'busy' is often more a mental phenomenon than a physical one. Your mind is crowded with information, constantly jumping ahead to the next thing instead of focusing on what's happening right now. And it's usually distracted every few moments by a ping or a beep or the pull of social media. We have all the technology and tools we need to get things done more quickly but, rather than allowing us to have more time and space in our lives, that efficiency means we cram even more into the time we have. We make calls from the car or send emails while waiting for coffee. Standing in line, riding on a bus or waiting for a friend could be opportunities for some mental downtime, but instead we instinctively pull out our phones and start swiping and scrolling. A busy mind creates a sense of urgency, a constant pulse of nervous energy, which makes it feel impossible to slow down. You tell yourself you don't have the luxury of taking a break right now, that you'll take a step back just as soon as you get through your to-do list or meet the next deadline.

Of course, that time never comes.

THE REAL COST OF BUSYNESS

We generally consider this state to be a sad fact of modern life. But the things I hear people complain about the most – stress, weight gain, insomnia, disconnected relationships, guilt and fatigue – can all be attributed, either directly or indirectly, to the maddening pace of life.

When you can't switch off your mind, you lie awake at night. Sleep deprivation is linked with depression and anxiety, as well as a long list of physical health risks including diabetes, obesity, hypertension, heart disease and even Alzheimer's disease. Being chronically busy can cause your body to overproduce the stress hormone cortisol. Too much cortisol can lead you to crave sugary foods that spike your blood sugar, which then quickly crashes back down. Overproduction of cortisol also disrupts your body's natural ability to regulate your hunger hormones – the ones that tell you when you're hungry and when you're full. Plus, when you're busy, you're probably grabbing snacks on the go and not being particularly mindful of how much you're consuming. Being constantly connected to devices means we are not present. We're not focused on what's happening right in front of us, including the people who would benefit the most from our full attention. Friendships move online, because there's not enough time to catch up in person, and the people you live with are all staring at screens instead of talking to each other.

You pride yourself on your ability to multi-task, but the research is clear: there is no way you can be actively doing more than one thing at any one time. What you are doing is constantly moving your attention between one thing and another. Task switching may give you the illusion that you're making progress, but not only is it highly inefficient, reducing your productivity by as much as 40 per cent, it also gradually reduces not only your capacity to control your attention, but even your IQ.

Constant skimming of articles, working among distractions and task switching causes you to lose your capacity for what author Cal Newport calls 'deep work': that is, to focus deeply on a cognitively demanding task without interruption. Doing deep work produces high-quality outcomes and is deeply fulfilling. Make no mistake: being *busy* and being *productive* are not the same thing.

THE CASE FOR SLOWING DOWN

The minute you quiet your busy mind, you allow space for creative and abstract thoughts to emerge. If you've ever had an idea come to you while you're out for a walk, having a shower or meditating, you'll know this. Coming up with new solutions to old problems requires a different kind of thinking: a kind of thinking that is innovative and open to a broad range of perspectives. This is called 'divergent' thinking, and it uses the neural circuitry that is activated when you're brainstorming ideas or daydreaming. It's what happens when you have flashes of intuition or light-bulb moments because you let your mind wander, put down the phone or stop ruminating on the problem. Usually, this is exactly what we need, and yet too often we convince ourselves that we don't have time for those breaks.

Slowing down in a world that glorifies being busy can feel like an act of rebellion.

Time is finite, but energy is renewable

We convince ourselves that we need to rush through life because we have limited time to get things done. But while time may be a finite resource, our energy is renewable. When we focus on doing things that replenish our physical and mental energy, we are far more likely to maximise the use of our available time. Research has proven that we can only remain focused on a task for around ninety minutes before we become distractible, losing concentration and making mistakes. Just as athletes schedule recovery into their training plans, we need to schedule breaks in our busy lives if we want to perform at our best. With unscheduled time, your body relaxes, your mind has the space to generate intuitive, creative thoughts, and the physiological processes that are damaged by chronic stress begin to return to healthy functioning.

Most importantly, unscheduled time allows you to reflect on what's truly important, and whether you are prioritising the activities that have the most potential to bring you joy. The greatest tragedy is when you are too busy chasing the things you *think* will make you happy to notice that real happiness is right here, and you're probably missing it. Every day is filled with opportunities for shared connection with the people you love, for savouring the beauty all around you and for enjoying and being grateful for everything you have, but as a society we have become so distracted and preoccupied that these opportunities pass us by, unnoticed.

What do you value?

Slowing down means being intentional about how you spend your time and energy. It means taking control of your schedule and ensuring that the activities that are of the greatest value to you are given the highest priority. Rather than always reacting to what is *urgent*, it means ruthlessly prioritising what is *important*.

And what is important must include time for rest and relaxation. Have you ever noticed that when you're stressed and overwhelmed, the things you know would have the greatest positive effect on your health and wellbeing are usually the first things you drop, because you 'don't have time'?

By saying no to others,
you are saying yes to
yourself.

We must ensure the trivial does not get in the way of the essential.

Start politely declining invitations and drop those voluntary commitments that are sucking the life out of you. Set firm boundaries to protect your physical and emotional energy. It will probably feel pretty uncomfortable at first. But when you know your frantic schedule is having a negative impact on your health and happiness, it's essential that you prioritise your own needs and the needs of your family. As Professor Brené Brown says, 'It takes courage to say yes to rest and play in a culture where exhaustion is seen as a status symbol.'

START SLOWING DOWN

Schedule downtime

If your calendar is so full that you feel exhausted just looking at it, take an honest appraisal of your commitments. How many of them are really necessary? What are you doing out of obligation? What can be delegated to someone else? If you have children, take a look at their schedules while you're at it. You want them to have every opportunity to fulfil their potential, but they also need unstructured time.

There will always be things we are required to do whether we like it or not, but there should also be time that is unscheduled. See if you can find the gaps in your diary (or create them), and pencil in some time to do nothing.

Unplug

How much of your mental busyness comes from being constantly connected to a device that's designed to hijack your attention and destroy your capacity to focus? Think about how much of your stress comes in the form of incoming emails, requests and messages that feel like they need an immediate response. Dedicate time to being phone-free, perhaps for an hour when you first get up in the morning and an hour before bed or during dinner. Ditch your device and savour the break from its never-ending attempts to hijack your attention and steal your peace of mind.

Pause with purpose

The fastest way to drop out of your busy, overthinking
mind is to tune in to your own breathing. Deep,
purposeful breathing deactivates the 'fight or flight'
response and activates a relaxation response instead.
Your stress levels fall. Your brain receives the message
that you're no longer in danger and dials down the
cortisol production, returning your system to balance.
Just three minutes of calm breathing, checking in with
your racing thoughts and loosening the tension in
your body, can go a long way towards keeping you in
a state that is calmer, less hurried and more present.
It stops you obsessively rushing through life to the
next thing and reconnects you to the present moment.
Schedule reminders in your phone throughout the day
to stop, breathe, observe, and then continue with your
day a little more mindfully.

Step three

LEARN TO LET GO

How much time have you spent being upset about things that are completely out of your control, like missing out on a job, crappy weather on your holiday, or getting caught in a traffic jam when you're late for an appointment?

And how often have you seethed about other people's behaviour, even though you know there's nothing you can do to change them?

We all experience our share of difficulty in life, from minor hurts and grievances all the way through to the dreaded Ds: divorce, disease and death of loved ones.

You are bound to experience adversity and emotional upheaval in your lifetime. This might vary in intensity from mildly irritating to utterly devastating, but what all these things have in common is that they can't be changed.

It's also true that some people experience a disproportionate amount of suffering. Life is not necessarily fair when it comes to dishing out difficulties, but we all have our own battles to face at some time or another. No-one gets a free pass, so the only thing that will bring you peace is to let go of the idea that things should somehow be different. It's the age-old wisdom of accepting what can't be changed. Of course, sometimes the simplest idea is the hardest to apply.

> **"Life is not necessarily fair when it comes to dishing out difficulties, but we all have our own battles to face at some time or another."**

Pain is the hard stuff you inevitably have to deal with in life. Pain is sometimes unavoidable. *Suffering* is the mental struggle you engage in when you have difficulty accepting life's painful events. Signs that you're having trouble with acceptance might include replaying events in your mind, stewing over how unfair or wrong something is, or how someone should or shouldn't have behaved. It's a tightness in your chest or a churning in your stomach. It might feel like righteous indignation or deep sorrow, or a longing for things to go back to the way they were. If you're feeling these things, it's fair to say you haven't learned to let go. The struggle sometimes feels like determined and justified resistance. At other times, it feels like a kicking, screaming toddler refusing to hear the word 'no'.

When you drop that struggle and let go of trying to control the uncontrollable, you tend to move out of your suffering far more quickly than you otherwise might. Then you can mobilise your resources to deal with the challenge, to do the things that will support you and the people around you, and to focus on the joy still to be found in life, rather than wasting valuable time and energy focusing on what can't be changed.

Pain is inevitable.
Suffering is optional.

All those years ago when Buddha reached enlightenment, his first teaching was that in life there is suffering. He also taught that the path out of suffering is to let go of our attachments: that is, our need for things to be somehow different from the way they are right now. The only thing any of us can truly be sure of is the impermanent nature of all things. In other words, the only constant in life is change. When things are going well for you, you hold on tight, wishing it could last forever. But when things are going wrong, you want nothing more than for that to stop.

When you stop wishing, hoping, bemoaning, blaming, justifying and hand-wringing, you claim back all that wasted energy. That's when you can fully immerse yourself in the joy that's to be found right here and now in this flawed, stressful, imperfect life.

If you can let go of your need for things to be a particular way in order for you to be happy, then you'll have a far greater chance of being happy.

ACCEPTANCE IS NOT DEFEAT

The biggest problem most people have with the idea of acceptance is that it feels a bit like throwing in the towel. Let's be clear: acceptance when used in this context is absolutely not the same as resignation. Acceptance doesn't mean that you don't still work to change the things you have the power to change. What it means is that you let go, once and for all, of the things that you can't change, put aside the idea that circumstances or people 'should' be different, and you *stop behaving as if your happiness depends on circumstances or people being different*. This is crucial.

"Acceptance doesn't mean that you don't still work to change the things you have the power to change."

When you choose to take the position of acceptance, what you are essentially saying is, 'Okay, so this is how things are. I may not like it and I certainly didn't invite it, but nonetheless, this is what I have to work with right now.' It truly can feel like a weight has been lifted when you accept that there's nothing to be gained from wishing things were different, pretending they are different or waiting for them to change. You can finally let go of your resistance and see things clearly, because *what other choice do you have?*

Sometimes people like to substitute the word 'willingness' for acceptance. Essentially, the words are interchangeable. In this context, willingness refers to you being willing to allow things to be as they are. It acknowledges that you are exercising a choice, and that can feel empowering when you're feeling helpless and at the mercy of events out of your control.

The willingness to accept painful emotions puts you back in charge of your choices.

FEEL YOUR FEELINGS

If only we could go through life without ever feeling sadness, loneliness, anger, fear, humiliation or grief. We know how unrealistic that is, but we still can't help thinking it would be nice. But to be human is to experience the whole gamut of human emotions – from exhilaration to despair and everything in between. Somewhere along the way, you might have adopted the view that 'negative' emotions are bad, and should be avoided. I think the positive thinking movement may be partly to blame for this idea, but I also know that it's sometimes instilled in us as children. You may have early memories of being told to cheer up, stop crying, there's nothing to be afraid of, you're being silly, get over it. You might have been punished for expressing anger. You might have internalised the idea that unpleasant emotions are unacceptable, and learned to shove those feelings down and not express them.

If you are unwilling or unable to sit with difficult thoughts and feelings, you'll have crafted all sorts of clever ways to 'opt out' of experiencing them. But just as trying to control your outer world is usually a fruitless exercise, so is trying to control your inner world. In Acceptance and Commitment Therapy, which is a mindfulness-based approach to the treatment of psychological suffering, efforts you make to 'fix' or avoid difficult thoughts and feelings are referred to as 'control strategies'. Control strategies ultimately become the problem, not the solution. Actively suppressing, avoiding or numbing difficult feelings only creates more distress in the long run. As the saying goes, what you resist persists.

> "Actively suppressing, avoiding or numbing difficult feelings only creates more distress in the long run."

To be clear, you will benefit in many ways by injecting more positive thoughts and feelings into your life. If I didn't believe that, I wouldn't be writing this book. But the curious paradox here is that attempts to rid your life of negative emotions often only serve to make those emotions more prevalent.

Have you ever turned to a family-sized block of chocolate or a bottle of wine to help take the edge off after a stressful day? Ever consoled yourself after a break-up with a fabulous pair of shoes? Occasionally treating yourself can be just the thing to help you through a rough time, but if you find that you're always running away from your feelings by running towards the instant gratification of food or alcohol or shiny new things, you may be creating more problems for yourself down the track. For example, let's say you soften your jagged emotional edges with a couple of drinks. No doubt you feel more relaxed. Later, though, you probably don't sleep as well as you normally would, and you might wake up feeling a bit lethargic. By starting it on the back foot, you are adding more stress to your day, making you more likely to feel depleted at the end of that day. And so the cycle continues.

The more often you do something that hits that reward centre in your brain (like alcohol or food or shopping does), the more likely you are to keep doing it. Your brain quickly creates neural pathways that reinforce behaviours that feel good, which is how those habits can turn into addictions. As the famous Samuel Johnson quote goes, 'The chains of habit are too light to be felt until they are too heavy to be broken.'

Meanwhile, you haven't processed those emotions at all, which means they're still there waiting to be dealt with, along with whatever remorse, anxiety or headache you might be experiencing thanks to your hangover or credit-card debt. It's also worth remembering that you cannot selectively numb your feelings. Whatever you might do to take the edge off your painful feelings will also blunt positive emotions like joy and gratitude.

There are plenty of other tricks you might use to opt out of your discomfort. Perfectionism is a strategy we use to avoid feeling like we're not good enough. Being endlessly busy means not having to sit with your thoughts for too long. Burying yourself in work is a great way to avoid dealing with problems at home. Persistently googling information, asking others' opinions and seeking reassurance are all strategies people use to reduce the uncomfortable tension of uncertainty. And, of course, anyone who experiences anxiety knows that the simplest control strategy is to avoid the things that scare you. By ducking and weaving and constantly seeking ways to avoid difficult or unpleasant emotions, you deny yourself the opportunity to discover that you can tolerate those feelings. Meanwhile, the more you try to limit your exposure to discomfort, the smaller your world becomes.

Letting go of control can feel difficult or frightening, but ultimately your happiness depends on your willingness to accept that some emotional discomfort in the short term leads to a happier and more fulfilling life in the long term. When you stop running from your feelings and turn to face what feels painful, knowing you are strong enough to survive it, you will experience a kind of freedom you might never have known before.

PRACTISE ACCEPTANCE

Register your resistance

Pay attention to the particular areas of your life where you struggle with acceptance. This could be a person or a situation; or it might be particular feelings you try to avoid, such as loneliness, boredom or anxiety. Also notice any situations that cause you to think, 'That's not fair', 'It shouldn't be like this' or 'Why me?', and especially be aware of any tendency to use the word 'should' in relation to circumstances beyond your control. Try to be impartial in your observation, and simply note the difficulty you have with acceptance.

Recognise your control strategies

Think about what kind of strategies you routinely use to control your outer world or your inner world. The greater your need for control and certainty, the greater the likelihood that you'll experience stress and anxiety, because the world is inherently uncertain. Do you micromanage the people around you? Do you seek reassurance by constantly asking for people's opinions? Or do you self-soothe with substances or shopping? Start loosening the grip of these habits and trying to turn towards difficulty, instead of running away from it.

Feel emotions in your body

Every emotion can be experienced as a bodily sensation. Anxiety might be a churning in your stomach. Sadness can feel heavy on your heart. When you're experiencing something painful, try to unhook from your thinking mind that wants to dwell on all the reasons this shouldn't be happening, and instead drop into those feelings in your body. Tuning in to physical sensations with curiosity and kindness is a great way to increase your capacity to tolerate discomfort. If you can stay with those feelings long enough, they usually have a way of passing by on their own.

Step four

BE KIND TO YOURSELF

As a psychologist and mindfulness teacher, I know that most people are plagued by harsh and unrelenting self-criticism.

You're probably no different. I recently realised that neither am I. I thought I had got better at accepting myself as I got older. I tend to speak my mind more and worry less about others' opinions than I did when I was younger. But one day I decided to pay particular attention to my own internal monologue. I was surprised by the barrage of judgemental commentary that commenced immediately and touched on just about every area of my life. My jeans were a bit tight (must lose weight), my kitchen bench was a mess (so disorganised), and I was behind in my admin at work (lazy). I was letting my daughter have too much screen time and not doing enough to get her to eat more vegetables (terrible parent). I had overdue bills to pay (financially irresponsible). On and on it went, the voice in my head nitpicking every aspect of my performance as a friend, mother, wife, householder and professional. The constant drone of self-criticism created a low-level tension that followed me around all morning.

I reflected that day on what it would take for me to be truly happy with myself, and it became obvious that I was striving for a level of perfection that probably doesn't exist. I'd need to be a perfect parent, keep an immaculate house, attend regular gym/Pilates/yoga classes, meditate every morning and cook only organic meals from scratch. Not to mention consume much less coffee and wine. I also realised that if I ever met that perfect person, I probably wouldn't want to be friends with her.

Perfectionism is, of course, the stablemate of self-criticism, except that perfectionism has a sneaky way of convincing you it's an admirable quality. You might even brag about what a perfectionist you are, but, in most cases, perfectionism is a form of fear. Specifically, it is the fear of not being good enough. Striving to hold yourself to a high standard because you take pride in your work, your appearance or your home is not the kind of perfectionism I'm talking about. I'm talking about making your standard impossibly high, and then evaluating your self-worth based on your failure to meet it.

We are all imperfect, and it's those imperfections that we embrace in other people because it makes them seem real and relatable. But revealing our own flaws is another matter altogether. Learning to let go of self-criticism and be a little kinder to yourself, especially when you feel like you don't deserve it, will go a long way towards boosting your happiness.

"We are all imperfect, and it's those imperfections that we embrace in other people because it makes them seem real and relatable."

It's hard to be happy
when someone is
being mean to you
all the time.

SELF-CRITICISM DOES NOT LEAD TO SELF-IMPROVEMENT

You may be under the illusion that it is only by being hard on yourself that you'll ever change or improve. I constantly hear people say that if they go easy on themselves, they'll just get lazy and never achieve anything. Research clearly indicates that this is not the case. People who are highly self-critical are much more likely to suffer from worry, stress, anxiety and depression, and are in fact *less* likely to achieve their goals. Ask yourself if being bullied or shamed has ever motivated you to do better. For most of us, the answer is no, and yet we assume that bullying and berating ourselves will have that effect.

Perfectionism won't allow you to progress towards your goals because nothing you do will ever be good enough. Perfectionism is thinking you need another qualification before you can open your business or charge for your services. It's not publishing your blog until you've re-edited it a dozen times. It's not applying for a job you want because you're not 100 per cent satisfied that you have all the credentials. Perfectionism often looks like procrastination, or getting all your ducks in a row before you take the first step towards a goal. It's seductive, because you can pass it off as just you being a high achiever, but deep down you know it is, as Elizabeth Gilbert says, 'just fear in a fancy coat'.

Thanks to advances in neuroscience, we now know that this tendency towards harsh self-judgement is at least partly due to how our brains are wired.

Wired for self-criticism

In the past few decades, there have been amazing advances in neuroscience that have taught us a great deal about how our brains work. One finding came about fairly accidentally, when people involved in a brain imaging study were taking a break between mental tasks. Researchers noticed that rather than their brains effectively going 'offline', they became even more active. Without a mental task to perform, the neural circuitry known as the 'default mode network' lights up. This brain activity reflects what most of us already know: when there isn't much else on our minds, we default to self-referential thinking. We humans are by nature fairly egocentric, consumed with our own concerns, objectives and problems. To be fair, some of this thinking is useful. It makes us socially responsible and guides us towards making ethical decisions.

The other part of our brain that comes online, which is not so helpful, is the part that focuses on finding problems or errors. The default mode network also leads us to imagine things that don't exist. This is great for brainstorming and coming up with new, innovative ideas, but it's not so great when you're thinking about yourself and finding problems. It can lead to judging yourself harshly and then assuming that other people are judging you too.

Stop comparing what you know about yourself with what you don't know about other people.

COMPARE AND DESPAIR

Comparing yourself to other people is human nature. Unfortunately, it can also be a great way of finding all the ways you don't measure up to the people around you. Back in the 1950s, a psychologist named Leon Festinger came up with a theory of social comparison, hypothesising that in the absence of any measurable indication of our own talent or skill, we look to the people around us to assess how well we're doing.

Upward comparison is when you measure yourself against someone you perceive is doing better than you. This can serve as inspiration, motivating you to work harder to achieve your goals. Downward comparison is when you compare yourself with those worse off. Ideally, this might make you feel more appreciative of what you have, or give you some perspective when you're feeling down on yourself.

The problem is, of course, that mainstream and social media have changed our field of comparison. We have unprecedented access to the lifestyles of the rich and famous, and, even among your 'regular' friends, the use of social media means that what you see is often a carefully crafted, edited and filtered version of real life. Being constantly exposed to the highlights of everyone else's lives when you're simultaneously preoccupied with everything that's wrong in your own life means comparison is very much the thief of joy.

When you engage in comparison and feel envious of what others are doing or achieving, it's because you believe if you had or did those things, you would be happier. You mistakenly believe that if you had a more stylish wardrobe, flawless skin or a bigger house, you'd be more satisfied with your life. But, as we've already established, those things have an almost inconsequential effect on happiness. Remind yourself that these are false assumptions, and guard against the temptation to believe them.

TRY A LITTLE SELF-COMPASSION

Practising self-compassion means being kind to yourself when you're suffering. Often, the reason you're suffering is your own perceived inadequacy, especially if things aren't going well. Psychologist Kristin Neff, who has done substantial research in this area, has found that practising self-compassion is the most effective antidote to harsh self-judgement. Contrary to the idea that you might be letting yourself off the hook, it's been proven that people who practise self-compassion are actually more likely to strive towards their goals, bounce back from setbacks and failures, and achieve what they want in life. Self-compassion is also associated with much lower rates of stress, anxiety and depression.

Those times that life throws you a curveball, that you take a risk and fail, that you experience rejection or disappointment, are the times you need to dig deep and find a well of patience, kindness and encouragement inside yourself. These are not the times for comparing or for berating yourself. They're times to treat yourself the way you would a good friend. This doesn't come naturally to many of us, and that's why you need to practise until you override that default mode and create a different neural pathway.

"Self-compassion doesn't come naturally to many of us, and that's why you need to practise until you override that default mode."

PRACTISE SELF-KINDNESS

Affirm your strengths

Some research shows that if you acknowledge within yourself the ways you are living in alignment with your values, this can have a powerful effect on your sense of self-worth. Rather than chanting empty affirmations, affirm your particular strengths and values. So for example, if you are a person who values being a good parent, you might acknowledge all the things you do for your kids, even when it's difficult or inconvenient. Keep looking for opportunities to recognise and validate your efforts to live by your values.

Accept compliments

Learning to be kinder to yourself also means accepting other people's kindness towards you. If someone says they admire something about you, or celebrates you for something you've achieved, catch yourself before you dismiss or minimise their kind words. Pause, take a breath and say, 'Thank you'. Start learning to acknowledge the things you do well and the personal qualities people tell you they admire the most. Train yourself, slowly but surely, to believe people when they pay you a compliment.

Discover the three key components

The three key components that Kristin Neff found are central to self-compassion are **mindfulness**, **common humanity** and **self-kindness**.

When you notice you're getting down on yourself, be aware of what's happening. What are the stories you're telling yourself? What are you feeling? Being mindful means observing your experience without getting swallowed up by it.

Next, remember that everyone feels this way sometimes. Everyone has that negative inner voice, and we all mess things up occasionally. Remembering our common humanity helps you get out of the comparison trap that tells you everyone else is doing better than you are.

And finally, extend kindness to yourself as an alternative to self-judgement. Offer yourself the same warmth and friendliness you would offer a friend.

Step five

THINK
HAPPIER
THOUGHTS

Have you ever noticed that if ten good things happen in a day and one bad thing, it's the bad thing that you'll remember?

We have so many opportunities to notice what's going well, but instead we zero in on the stuff that makes us feel crappy. Sometimes we go as far as making up reasons to feel anxious or miserable. We anticipate all the worst-case scenarios, or make false assumptions about what other people are thinking about us. All of this unhelpful thinking is caused by your brain's negativity bias, which leads you to focus much more intensely on what's going wrong than on what's going well. Of course, noticing problems and being alert to potential danger is what's kept us safe throughout history, so we can thank evolution for this bias.

The problem is that as soon as your mind gets hold of a negative thought, this quickly creates a downward spiral. One thought leads to another, and then another. This chain of unhelpful thoughts creates unpleasant emotions, and once you're in a bad mood, you're more likely to interpret situations through that negative lens. Imagine you text a friend and she seems a little curt in her reply. If you're already feeling low, you're more likely to jump to the conclusion that perhaps you've done something to upset her. As your mind focuses on this idea, you feel tense, anxious and preoccupied.

> **"Once you're in a bad mood, you're more likely to interpret situations through that negative lens."**

You start rehashing your recent conversations, looking for clues to what might have annoyed her. Part of you knows you're being irrational, but instead of shaking it off, you chastise yourself for being so neurotic. You wonder why you can't just be normal and easygoing like other people.

It's easy to see that if you don't take control of your thoughts, this cascade of negativity happens very automatically. These negative assumptions make your bad mood a hundred times worse. You might then choose to cancel your plans to go out, and instead stay home watching Netflix and eating ice-cream because you're 'not very good company'. Now, instead of feeling better, you're feeling even more alone. It's a vicious, self-defeating, miserable cycle.

Breaking the negativity loop means first becoming aware of it.

BREAKING THE HABIT

Just like in that previous scenario, most of the thinking you do is very habitual and automatic. The whole purpose of habits is that they don't require any concentrated effort on your part. They bypass the part of your brain that's involved in conscious decision-making and planning, freeing up brain space for more important things. Every day you have at least 60,000 thoughts, and most of these thoughts will be the same ones you had yesterday and that you'll have again tomorrow.

"Every day you have at least 60,000 thoughts, and most of these thoughts will be the same ones you had yesterday and that you'll have again tomorrow."

This means that every day, you are interpreting situations and reacting to people and events using heavily entrenched patterns of thinking, many of which are negative or self-defeating.

Simply notice and acknowledge how frequently you default to the kinds of thoughts that affect your mood in a negative way. If you can do this without self-judgement, you're beginning to practise the skill of mindfulness. Being mindful means that as you are having an experience (whether a thought, feeling, urge or physical sensation), you are aware of it and can make a more considered choice about what to do next. If you are aware that you're going down a well-worn path of negativity, you can choose to pause before you go any further. With mindfulness, you can learn to let go of those unhelpful thoughts and stop allowing them to hijack your mood. This new level of awareness then means you can go one step further and seek out opportunities to practise a more positive way of thinking, enabling you to replace those old habits with something that will make you feel less crappy and more happy.

THE POWER OF POSITIVITY

Unpleasant emotions grab your attention and narrow your focus, compelling you to dwell on a problem. Whether you're experiencing fear, sadness, anger or guilt, your mind will zero in on whatever is causing you to feel that way in order to try and fix it. When you feel stressed, anxious or upset, you turn your attention inward, become preoccupied with your worries and withdraw from the world around you.

What we know about the function of positive emotions, thanks largely to the work of Professor Barbara Fredrickson, is that, by contrast, they broaden your perspective and turn your attention outward. When you feel joy, you have the urge to reach out to people. You're more optimistic about the future and more likely to see opportunities in the world around you. When your curiosity is piqued (another positive emotion), you're driven to learn, study, explore and seek out new information, further developing your knowledge and skills. When you feel pride in your achievements you might be inspired to reach for even higher goals, thus challenging yourself to grow and develop.

"When you're in an optimistic and positive state, you forge social bonds, create happy memories and set yourself meaningful goals."

Professor Fredrickson called this the 'Broaden and Build' theory of positive emotions, because the more you focus on increasing your positivity, the more you *broaden* your perspective and *build* your personal resources. When you're in an optimistic and positive state, you forge social bonds, create happy memories and set yourself meaningful goals. These resources then help you to bounce back from setbacks. In many ways, your resilience is cultivated as much by your positive experiences as it is by your negative ones.

Since negative experiences leave a sticky emotional residue, it takes at least three positive experiences to counteract the effects of just one negative one.

How to be more positive

Practising positivity is not about pasting on a smile and pretending things are okay when they're not, and it certainly doesn't mean denying, suppressing or avoiding your own painful feelings. We've established that to be human is to experience the full range of emotions. What you don't need, though, is to create problems in your own mind or give undue attention to the negative while ignoring all the opportunities to feel good. Practising positivity is intended to counteract the negativity bias that continually steers your mind towards what's wrong.

Unpleasant experiences are easy to spot – they include everything from the stress of running late for work to the mounting pile of bills and the daily hassles of life. Then there's the big stuff: illness, ageing, divorce and death. When it comes to shifting the balance so that the positive outweighs the negative, one of the first things you can do is to actively reduce the amount of negativity you are allowing into your life.

Let's take a quick inventory of some of the most obvious sources of negativity. Firstly, there is negative media. The evening news is a highlights reel of every disastrous, traumatic, painful thing that has happened in the past twenty-four hours. If you get your news from social media, you're not confined to a 6 pm timeslot for your daily dose of misery. You can get a fix every time you pick up your device. Then there are negative people. The friends and colleagues who only ever want to complain or offload their troubles onto you, or the toxic people who actively seek to aggravate or undermine you. There are the social media accounts that make you feel bad about yourself because they present a false image of perfection that you'll never achieve. Remove what you can and do your best to limit your exposure to anything or anyone that you can't completely avoid. Take charge of your space and be unapologetic in your quest to reduce the negative energy in your life.

From thoughts
come feelings
and from feelings
come thoughts.

STOP FEEDING THE BEAST

It's proven that emotions are contagious. And sometimes, like any other contagious condition, you can transfer them back and forth, meaning you're always getting a dose. This often happens in workplaces when a small group of unhappy campers create what's called the 'rotten apple' effect, spreading their negative attitude to their colleagues. Once you've taken steps to reduce the amount of negative energy in your life, it's time to assess how much of that negativity you are putting out or actively engaging in. Sometimes it can be fun to gossip about someone, or whinge about your boss or partner. But there is a difference between talking to someone who will listen impartially and offer you support, and indulging in petty complaining, judging and criticising. Negativity breeds more negativity. If you are focusing heavily on what's wrong and you find someone who will feed your story with their own negative thoughts and feelings, it will spread like a virus. You might start off feeling better because someone understands, but unless you focus on how to make a positive change you will wind up feeling much worse.

> **"It's your responsibility to manage your own space, and also to be mindful of your contribution to others'."**

Not only that, but your negativity is draining the emotional energy of those around you. It's your responsibility to manage your own space, and also to be mindful of your contribution to others'. Put yourself into quarantine and refuse to be part of the negative contagion.

Happiness
is contagious.
Spread it!

LOSE THE NEGATIVITY

Quit complaining

Challenge yourself to go twenty-four hours without complaining, and notice how often your mind automatically slips into finding fault. If you become aware that you have a habit of complaining that's hard to break, extend your complaint detox to a week or a month – you'll feel the difference.

Lead with curiosity

When we come across people who are unpleasant or who behave in a way we don't agree with, we often make snap judgements, take the moral high ground or assume these people are rude, arrogant or thoughtless. Instead, try wondering what might be going on in their lives. What kinds of things might have led them to behave in this way? What might they be going through? Give people the benefit of your kindness and generosity of spirit, instead of your judgement and criticism.

Get out of the blame game

Take responsibility for your own happiness. What's happened to you in the past may not be your fault, but your future is your responsibility. It is possible to offer yourself compassion without making yourself a victim. Notice if you are always looking to find someone or something to blame for your crappy mood or crappy life. It is far more empowering to take control of what you can, let go of what you can't and embrace your future with positivity.

PRACTISE POSITIVITY

Be grateful

Several studies have shown that placing deliberate attention on what you feel grateful for has a positive and lasting impact on your mood. You might decide to keep a gratitude journal, listing three things each day that you feel deep appreciation for. You might write a thank-you note to someone who has helped you out. Taking note of the positive things in your life causes you to start looking for the things you feel grateful for.

Savour joy

To savour an experience means squeezing every drop of goodness out of it. It means paying attention to your feelings, noticing the curve of the smile on your lips or the twinkle of joy lighting up a child's eyes as they tell you something they're excited about. Notice how happiness feels in your body. Savouring a moment means immersing yourself completely and soaking it up at a visceral level. Unlike mindfulness, which is about being fully present in this moment, you can savour happy memories or even savour the anticipation of something you're looking forward to.

Be kind

Being kind will make you feel happier, increase your engagement with people, and improve your outlook on the world. Even if the only thing you have to offer is a smile or a compliment, the gift of kindness is one of the most valuable things you can give. Several studies have found that spending money on other people or on charitable causes has a far more positive impact on your mood than spending money on yourself. This is called 'prosocial spending', and is consistently linked with happiness.

Step six

FIND YOUR
PEOPLE

Hundreds of thousands of years ago, when humans roamed the African savanna as hunter-gatherers, they relied on their tribe for food, companionship and safety.

To be rejected by the group was to be left for dead. As a result, the need for belonging and social acceptance has been bred into our DNA.

In today's world, we may not be endangered by the elements, predators or hostile tribes, but we still very much rely on social connections for our physical and mental wellbeing.

"Loneliness and social isolation have been proven to be as toxic to your health as cigarette smoking."

Intuitively, we all know the value of deep, lasting connections, but did you know that the quality of your relationships is in fact the single biggest predictor of your health and happiness in your later years? Loneliness and social isolation have been proven to be as toxic to your health as cigarette smoking. By definition, social isolation refers to having limited contact with people, whereas loneliness is the inner experience of feeling lonely. It's possible to feel lonely even in a crowd of people.

The famous Harvard Study of Adult Development (the Grant Study) is currently the world's longest-running research project, examining every aspect of men's lifestyles, health and wellbeing across the lifespan. The study began with 286 Harvard sophomores in 1938 and has continued for eighty years, later including the men's spouses and children. What the data collected makes abundantly clear is that relationships are the cornerstone of physical and emotional wellbeing.

George Vaillant is the Harvard psychiatrist who directed the study from 1972 to 2004. He is reported as saying that the most important finding to come from the research is that 'the only thing that matters in life is relationships'. In fact, participants' satisfaction with their relationships at age fifty was a stronger predictor of health in their eighties than their cholesterol levels. Happy marriages, long-term friendships and community involvement all keep people mentally and physically well.

People need people. We all share a basic human need to feel a sense of belonging, to have people who appreciate us for who we are and to know that there's someone we can count on to be there both in times of crisis and in times of celebration. The nature of the relationship doesn't matter, but the quality of the connection does.

STRENGTHENING CONNECTIONS

The key ingredient in quality relationships is time. It takes time to cultivate trust and intimacy, and it takes time for relationships to move from acquaintance to friend and then to close friend. Even when relationships are going well, we often don't give them the time and attention they really need to thrive. This might be because we're just too busy, or because we're unaware of just how important they are to our wellbeing.

How often do you prioritise other things over the important people in your life? Have you ever cancelled on a friend because of a work deadline? Ever rushed a conversation with your partner so you can get back to watching your favourite TV show? These days, a lot of our communication with friends has drifted to interactions through social media, or brief text messages. Sometimes we don't even bother with actual words; we use emojis as a substitute. This is all standard practice in our busy, hyper-connected lives, but it's worth examining how we're engaging with the people who matter most to us. You have to wonder whether sending that email *right now* is more important than sitting down and spending five uninterrupted minutes with your child or partner.

It can be hard to find the time, I know. We are all in the same *busy* boat, after all. A good friend will always understand, but when relationships are neglected for too long, they eventually wither and die. We tell ourselves that 'these things happen'; that our lives moved in different directions, or that physical distance makes it hard to stay connected. But the truth is, it's our own lack of care and attention that causes relationships to suffer – not distance or differing life choices, but neglect.

QUALITY NOT QUANTITY

Of course, time is a finite resource. If relationships require our time in order to survive and thrive, then it stands to reason that we need to choose where we invest that time wisely. It might be cool to keep adding friends on Facebook, but according to British anthropologist, evolutionary psychologist and author Robin Dunbar, you can only maintain any kind of meaningful relationship with around 150 people. That includes friends, family, colleagues and acquaintances. When it comes to your 'inner circle', that is, the people you could count on in a crisis, that number reduces to an average of three to five people.

After you've culled extraneous activities and reorganised your schedule, you'll probably find you still have limited time to invest in maintaining relationships. Therefore, by necessity, you might have to be a little ruthless. If you are trying to maintain too many connections, you could be doing yourself and your friends a disservice, because those are not the optimal conditions for relationships to thrive.

The inner circle:
5 close relationships

The next circle:
15 good friends

The outer circle:
50 friends

The full circle:
150 relationships

Imagine concentric circles expanding around you, with your five very closest relationships (including your partner, if you have one) in the inner circle with you. The next circle contains fifteen people you'd call good friends. These are the people you might regularly hang out with on the weekend. A full 75 per cent of your available time is spent on these fifteen people. The next circle (including the people in the first two) includes around fifty people you might count as friends. These might be the people you'd invite to a party, if you were having one. And finally, 150 is the maximum number of people you can keep any kind of meaningful relationship with. This is famously known as 'Dunbar's number', and he believes it hasn't changed much from our hunter-gatherer days. Even in this age of social media, where we can grow our friend count to the thousands, we only meaningfully engage with a very small number of those people.

SOCIAL MEDIA ISN'T VERY SOCIAL

I'll be the first to admit that I love social media. When I moved interstate three times in seven years, leaving good friends behind each time, I thought Facebook was the most amazing tool, because it enabled me to stay in touch with people in distant places. What I know now is that social media gives you the *illusion* of connection, which potentially reduces your motivation to make a real connection. When you see what your friends are doing, watch their kids grow and engage in brief online chats, you feel as if you're in touch with their day-to-day lives. But the danger of that illusion, in my opinion, is that when you feel the urge to connect with someone and then you see photos of their holidays or their kids online, your mind kind of 'ticks them off', even though you haven't connected with them in any meaningful way at all.

Feeling like you know what's happening in people's lives means you're less inclined to prioritise face-to-face time. It's a little bit like when you feel overwhelmed, so you write a to-do list. The act of writing the list feels good. It takes the pressure off and feels like you've achieved something, thus reducing your motivation to actually do any of the things on the list! I suspect something similar happens with online connections.

Only when you sit face-to-face with someone do you have the opportunity to really know what's on their mind and in their heart, beyond the polished, edited highlights reel you see on social media. You are also more likely to open up and share the truth about yourself when you connect with someone in person. Forming deep and lasting connections with people requires us to slow down and be really present with them; to put away distracting devices and listen fully; to notice the subtle nuances of facial expressions and gestures, not just the words being spoken.

Have you ever spent time with someone who seems more interested in taking photos on their phone than being present in the moment? Feeling like your company is only valued for its social shareability is a great way to destroy an opportunity for connection. Interestingly, the mere presence of a phone during a conversation has been shown to reduce trust and intimacy between people, so remember to put that phone away and look people in the eyes.

Social media gives
you the illusion of
connection. Be careful
not to mistake it for
the real thing.

ENDING TOXIC RELATIONSHIPS

Anything that has the potential to cause great joy can equally be the source of our greatest unhappiness. Sometimes people affect your life in a negative way; perhaps they don't contribute anything of value, drain your time and energy or actively seek to undermine you or diminish your feelings of self-worth. Fake friends can barely feign happiness when you achieve success. They take subtle digs at you, causing you to question your own value. Some people have a way of bringing out the worst in you. Your behaviour is your own responsibility, but if someone has a way of goading you into gossip or criticism, or brings out the mean-spirited, petty-minded aspects of your personality, I would suggest that you remove or limit contact with them.

It is important to weed any non-friends from your life to make room for more mutually supportive relationships. There is a saying that you become the average of the five people you spend the most time with.

"Have a look around at the company you're keeping and decide right now if you need to raise the quality of your crowd in order to be the best version of yourself."

Have a look around at the company you're keeping and decide right now if you need to raise the quality of your crowd in order to be the best version of yourself. There's no need for dramatic exits; you simply need to start moving away from the negative and toxic influences and investing more of your time in nurturing the relationships that are positive and mutually supportive.

Relationship rescue

If a relationship that is important to you has been neglected, this is easily resolved by shifting priorities and locking in some social engagements. But sometimes relationships turn sour for other reasons. Even among very good friends, disappointment, resentment, hurt feelings and miscommunication can erode a relationship to the point where it cannot be salvaged. As children, many of us weren't taught the skills to have difficult conversations or resolve conflict, so when problems arise, we can feel ill-equipped to deal with them. We become upset and withdrawn, unsure how to communicate how we feel. We might dig our heels in and stubbornly wait for the other person to apologise, or we might simply walk away, because it's easier than having a tough conversation.

If a relationship matters to you and you've invested years building trust, sharing your life and creating memories with someone, it's important to be willing to drop your defences (and your pride), allow yourself to be vulnerable and attempt to build that bridge. As we grow older, it can get harder to meet and connect with people or to move from being a casual acquaintance to a close friend. If you've already done the hard yards establishing intimacy and trust, it's worth taking a moment to consider whether you really want to throw that all away.

MAKE YOUR RELATIONSHIPS WORK

Be yourself

A true sense of belonging comes from knowing you are accepted for who you are, and that requires each of us to feel comfortable being ourselves, not projecting an ideal image in order to 'fit in' with a crowd. Professor Brené Brown discusses the difference between fitting in and belonging in her book *Braving the Wilderness*: 'Fitting in ... is assessing situations and groups of people, then twisting yourself into a human pretzel in order to get them to let you hang out with them. Belonging is something else entirely – it's showing up and letting yourself be seen and known as you really are.'

Be available

Relationships will die very quickly without an investment of time. Of course we all have those dear, long-term friends we can call on after a long absence and simply pick up where we left off, but those friendships have already benefited from a significant investment in our earlier lives (and they are still not immune to neglect). Ensuring that relationships continue to deepen and thrive requires us to put aside other demands and make ourselves available to spend quality time with the people who matter.

Be present

Small screens are the greatest threat to human connection. Our devices are addictive, and they can undermine the quality of our relationships in many ways. Make a concerted effort to ditch your device when in the company of people you care about. Remember, it is your relationships, over and above any other factor, that predict your quality of life as you age.

Step seven

DETERMINE
YOUR
DIRECTION

One of the biggest reasons people feel bored and uninspired in life is that they don't have any personally meaningful goals they are working towards.

Life can feel a bit 'Groundhog Day' when you get up day after day, week after week, just going through the motions. Ever had a whole year go by and realise you're basically in exactly the same spot you were before? It feels deflating and even depressing. If the scale of life satisfaction ranges from mental illness at one end of the spectrum to truly thriving at the other end, many people find themselves in the sub-par state known as 'languishing', which is just a little bit below even a moderate, 'average' level of mental health. In other words, you're not really depressed, but you're certainly not optimising your potential for success and happiness.

Meaningful goals give you a sense of purpose and direction that fuels and motivates you. As a coach, I often meet people who have trouble knowing where to start, or what their goals might be. If you've been meandering for a while, allowing yourself to be carried along by life rather than actively determining your destiny, it can be incredibly difficult to reconnect with the things that matter to you. But reconnect you must.

Striving towards personally meaningful goals is one of the critical ingredients in the happiness formula. But before you begin setting goals, it's important that we address some of what we know to be true about goals and goal striving, and how this relates to your happiness and wellbeing.

Making progress towards something that matters to you, whether it's saving for the trip of a lifetime, slogging your way through a university degree, or training for your first long-distance running event, usually feels difficult but worth it. You know there's going to be a great reward for all your effort.

> **"Have you ever achieved something you've worked hard for, only to find yourself feeling flat and a little depressed shortly afterwards?"**

But have you ever achieved something you've worked hard for, only to find yourself feeling flat and a little depressed shortly afterwards? I know it happened to me after I finished my senior year of high school, and again when I finished my first university degree. I remember almost counting the days to achieving those milestones, and then feeling completely untethered soon after.

There are many reasons for this, including what Harvard lecturer and author Tal Ben-Shahar calls 'Arrival Fallacy'. This is the mistaken belief that when you reach some future destination you'll sustain happiness. It's the very definition of the 'I'll be happy when ...' problem.

Of course, achieving goals feels fantastic, but if you're only focusing on the outcome, you're denying yourself all the joy that's yours to be had during those days, weeks, months and even years of working towards it. Your life is happening right now, in this moment. What a tragedy to postpone happiness until some day in the future – *especially* if you finally reach that goal and it feels like an anticlimax. Feeling engaged and purposeful, pushing yourself to grow and achieve something of value to you is a great source of personal satisfaction, and all of this is happening during the striving. So yes, absolutely, savour that moment when your effort pays off and you cross the finish line. Celebrate your success, because you deserve it. Just remember to also appreciate the process of getting there.

When it comes to happiness, the striving is often more important than the actual goal achievement.

CHOOSING THE RIGHT GOALS

The other important thing to know about goals and goal striving is that to be happy, you need to be working towards the 'right' goals. I use quotation marks because obviously there is no such thing as a right or wrong goal (unless you have morally questionable goals in mind!), but there are some goals that are proven to enhance your wellbeing. In other words, choosing the 'right' kind of goals in which to invest your time, resources and energy can make an enormous difference to your happiness. So let's talk about which kinds of goals are linked to happiness and which ones definitely are not.

Ever indulged in a fantasy about enjoying an extravagant, wealthy lifestyle? You're not alone. We all know those celebrities probably have bad days just like the rest of us; but you can't help thinking those struggles would be easier to deal with if you had an extra $50 million in the bank and a nanny, a driver, a chef and a personal assistant to help get you through.

The research on this is pretty clear. Aspiring to achieve wealth, status and fame is not the way to a fulfilling life. Of course, living in poverty is associated with less happiness, but beyond a certain level of income (enough to cover your basic expenses and have a little left over), adding extra zeros to your bank account doesn't substantially increase your happiness or wellbeing.

Some goals are what we refer to as extrinsically motivating or rewarding. These are the goals tied to external markers of success, such as material wealth, luxury goods, high status or public profile, accolades and awards. It's not that you can't be happy if you have these things. It's that *expecting* these things to bring you lasting joy and making them your main focus will not necessarily have the effect you want. This is because these kinds of goals have you always looking outwards for happiness or validation. The goals that are most likely to make you happy are the intrinsically rewarding ones. These are the things you can't see on the outside, such as human connection, being of service to others, learning new skills or fulfilling your potential. These kinds of goals have you looking to your own inner experience for fulfilment and satisfaction.

"Pursuing likes or followers on social media won't give you a feeling of connectedness to other people, much like increasing your net worth doesn't offer you a sense that you're making the world a better place."

Pursuing likes or followers on social media won't give you a feeling of connectedness to other people, much like increasing your net worth doesn't offer you a sense that you're making the world a better place. Where is your focus? Often as we get older, those intrinsically rewarding goals become more important as we realise that we've spent years chasing the things we thought would make us happy, only to find that they don't.

What I want to make abundantly clear here is that you can have wealth and fame and you may well be very happy, but that happiness will likely come not from the money or the fame. It's more likely to come from doing work you find personally meaningful, from giving back to the community or enhancing the lives of other people, or from feeling that you are achieving your potential. The money and the fame in those cases is often a by-product of your goal achievement, rather than being the main focus of your efforts. Some of the world's wealthiest people are, I'm sure, very happy because they are making a difference in other people's lives or using their platform to raise awareness of important social issues, and are no doubt having fun along the way. I doubt any of them would say that their wealth or celebrity status is their greatest source of joy.

By all means, let's set goals. But let's also step back and remember that there's already so much to be grateful for in our very mundane, imperfect and messy lives.

WHAT MATTERS MOST?

The most important thing about your goals is that they are personally meaningful to *you*. They must be aligned with your values; that is, what you hold as deeply important and what you want *your* life to be about. Happiness comes from striving towards goals that reflect your values, so, when reviewing your goals or setting new ones, it's important that you know what matters most to you in life. Other people's goals and aspirations aren't better or more worthwhile than your own, and your goals should absolutely not be determined by what you think other people want for you. There is no place for 'should' when it comes to deciding which goals to pursue in your life.

Two good friends who enjoy keeping fit together may have two very different motivations. One might want the satisfaction of completing a marathon while the other wants to lose the weight she gained during pregnancy and improve her stamina to keep up with two young children. They may both enjoy the companionship and the health benefits of running together, but ultimately they are working on very different, but personally meaningful goals.

For the past few years, I've been doing more of my work online. Every day, when I tune in to social media or open my email I'm bombarded with sales messages that promise me my happiness will arrive in the form of a seven-figure business. (A mere six-figure income is so passé.) These kinds of messages, along with the ones that try to convince me I need a 'bikini body' or a miracle anti-ageing cream to truly be happy, are always there, infiltrating my mind both consciously and subconsciously. These are all examples of extrinsically motivating goals, and I know they absolutely will not lead to sustained happiness. Even so, it takes determined effort to resist the pull of those messages and come back to choosing goals that will nourish your soul and give you a deep sense of fulfilment and purpose.

If you are more than happy on your solid five-figure income, paying your bills and working hours that suit your family, there is no shame in not wanting to 'hustle' to earn more. If you love your job, there is no rule that says you need to be doing something more 'extraordinary' to be truly happy or to have a meaningful life.

GOLDEN RULES FOR GOAL SETTING

Set both short- and long-term goals

Having a long-range plan for your life is important, but it's hard to stay motivated when the outcome you're working towards is so far in front of you it's barely a speck on the horizon. It keeps life interesting and challenging if you also have short- and medium-term goals. You might be working towards a holiday, a creative project and a career goal all at once. Bigger goals should also have smaller milestones, so you can track your progress.

Create multiple pathways

Maximising your confidence to achieve a goal involves having the will to achieve it along with multiple ways. If one path to your goal reaches a dead end, you want to be able to take a detour and find another way to get there. If you get too fixated on one route to your destination, it can be particularly discouraging if things don't work out. Try to keep your options open and not hold on too tightly to a preconceived idea about *how* you will reach your goal. Remember that most of your satisfaction comes from goal striving, not achievement.

Just keep swimming

Making progress towards goals is rarely a linear process. Along the way, you'll lose momentum, get sidetracked and become ambivalent. That is all normal, and is no reason to give up or to consider your efforts a failure. If there is something you want to achieve in life and you have a slip-up or setback along the way, simply be kind to yourself, hit the reset button and learn any lessons that might be there to help you avoid the same mistake in the future.

Step eight

GET OUT OF YOUR OWN WAY

If you've ever set out to achieve something and then done something that completely undoes your progress, you'll know firsthand the frustration of self-sabotage.

The infuriating part is that there doesn't seem to be any rational reason you would behave in this way. Therefore, you conclude that the problem is obviously you. You lack commitment or discipline. You're flaky or irresponsible. If our inner critic ever needed some material to work with, then here it is. Because why would any intelligent person act in ways that undermine their opportunity to succeed?

Sometimes you sabotage yourself in ways that don't seem intentional at all. Things like *accidentally* forgetting to put fuel in the car when you're supposed to be driving somewhere important, or leaving your wallet at home when it's time to put a deposit on a big purchase.

To understand this, you need to recognise the power of the subconscious mind. You see, all the thoughts you are aware of, the decisions you make and the goals you set are created with your conscious mind. These are the thoughts, plans, memories, worries and fantasies that you are very much aware of. But your conscious mind accounts for only around 5 per cent of all of the thoughts that influence your behaviour, while a whopping 95 per cent of your beliefs, ideas and emotions are operating at an unconscious level. By definition, this means they are completely out of your awareness. Our subconscious mind is very powerful and will trip you up, sometimes quite literally, if you don't understand its influence.

Your conscious thoughts are the tip of the iceberg. Self-sabotage is caused by what's happening beneath the surface.

LIMITING BELIEFS

Most of your core beliefs (that is, ideas you hold to be true about yourself, other people and the world) are not formed by someone telling you directly how things are, but rather by the messages you internalise from your experiences and observations. If you were nurtured as an infant, you internalised the message that you are lovable. If you were neglected or shamed, you probably absorbed a different message. Your experiences taught you whether the world is a safe place and whether people can be trusted.

In your family group, you might have received messages about your role in that group or about your potential in life. You might have absorbed the message that you're the pretty one or the sporty one, but not the smart one. On a societal level, many of the issues women face with poor body image are to do with what we've learned about the ideal beauty standard for women (hint: young, thin, flawless), combined with what women are most valued for in our society (hint: how they look). We internalise messages about what we are capable of, not just as individuals but as a consequence of our gender, race or sexual identity.

Money is an emotionally charged topic that people very often have subconscious beliefs about. Think about the messages you received about money or wealth when you were younger, and notice how they might be affecting your relationship with money now. Expressions like 'filthy rich' or 'money is the root of all evil' can have a powerful and lasting effect.

Because they aren't conscious, these ideas have never been held up to scrutiny, so they operate just outside your awareness, influencing how you behave. If you're feeling frustrated by your self-sabotaging behaviour, it's unlikely that you'll work out what's going on using your usual, conscious, problem-solving mind. To get to the bottom of it, you might have to do a little mental excavation and see if you can work out what's beneath the surface.

To simplify, I want to talk about the two most likely culprits undermining your efforts to succeed: fear of failure, and fear of success.

FEAR OF FAILURE

In sports psychology, self-handicapping is the term used when athletes sabotage their own performance. It describes acting in a way that gives you a built-in excuse for failing. If you were to give 100 per cent to achieving something of great importance to you, and you failed to achieve it, that would be painful, and potentially damaging to your sense of self. So to protect your self-esteem and your reputation, you do something that deliberately limits the likelihood of your own success. That way if you fail, you can blame your excuse and not your ability.

Outside of sports, self-sabotage might look like going out drinking the night before a big job interview or exam, so that if you mess up, you can blame your hangover (or alternatively, if you don't mess it up you can brag that you nailed it even with no sleep and little preparation).

Perfectionism strikes again

Sometimes what people call fear of failure is actually the fear of not achieving absolute success on the first attempt. In this case, it's the *definition* of failure and your unreasonable expectations that are the real problem. Succeeding at anything often involves multiple trials, evaluations, resets and pivots before you hit upon the winning formula. When it comes to changing a habit or behaviour like smoking or drinking, it's proven that people make multiple attempts to quit before that change is sustained. People often say they've tried so many times to reach a goal that they don't have it in them to try again. What they really mean is they have hit a setback and given up, and they are afraid of starting again because they might hit another setback. They will. This is not failure. It's life.

FEAR OF SUCCESS

It seems absurd that you might be afraid of the very thing you are working so hard to achieve. But it's worth considering whether something like this might be at play. Being afraid to succeed means that at some level you perceive there will be a negative consequence or unacceptable trade-off if you achieve what you want.

If you're a writer and your blog reaches more readers, you might become the target of online trolls. If you advance in your career you might be concerned about taking on extra responsibility, leaving behind your current

> **"If you advance in your career you might be concerned about taking on extra responsibility, leaving behind your current work team or longer work hours impacting your personal life."**

work team, or longer work hours affecting your personal life. If you lose a lot of weight, you might become the target of unwanted attention. World-renowned trauma therapist Bessel van der Kolk recounts an example of this in his book, *The Body Keeps the Score*. He reports that in an obesity clinic in the USA, clinicians were puzzled when a woman who had successfully shed 276 pounds (125 kilograms) on a weight-loss program went on to gain 37 pounds (16 kilograms) in one month after being sexually propositioned by a married male colleague. They later learned that the woman had been sexually abused as a child. When she became the target of unwelcome sexual attention, the weight piled on immediately because her subconscious mind had determined that 'overweight is overlooked' (and therefore safe). Understanding the negative consequence or the trade-off for your success is essential for getting to the cause of your self-sabotaging behaviours.

Tribal shame

Dr Mario Martinez is a clinical neuropsychologist who wrote a book called *The Mind Body Code*, in which he referred to the power of tribal shaming to hold people back from achieving their potential. We've established that we are social beings who are wired to belong to a community. Our first 'tribe' is our family, but a tribe might be any community you identify with, such as a religious group, workplace or political party. Basically, tribes have rules, even if they are unspoken, and rules violations can lead to rejection. Social rejection lights up the same areas of the brain as physical pain. This is because throughout history our very survival has required us to be part of a group.

Dr Martinez explains that if you act in ways that violate the tribal rules or norms, you will be shamed for your choices. For example, if your family is full of doctors and you want to be an artist, that might be considered unacceptable. If your family are all alcoholics and you choose not to drink, they might shame you for believing you're 'better than them'. Our undeniable need for social belonging and approval is so powerful that it often leads people to fail in their endeavours so that they can once again be embraced by the tribe. This is a key point in the tribal shame theory. The tribe will always embrace you and welcome you back into the fold if you fail.

Self-compassion
is the path to progress
so forgive yourself
for your slip-ups
and move on.

You may consciously tell yourself these things don't matter to you, that you want something different for yourself or your life, but if the part of the brain responsible for keeping you safe suspects you'll be shamed and rejected by your tribe, it will do everything it can to keep you from taking that risk.

OVERCOME SELF-SABOTAGE

Look for patterns

Reviewing your personal history can help you spot ways you have repeatedly tripped yourself up when you were working towards something important to you. What do your patterns tell you about what you think you're worthy of, or capable of? Do your self-defeating behaviours show up in your romantic life, your financial management or your career? Notice if there are themes that cut across more than one area. For example, does your self-sabotage usually stem from people pleasing, or from your difficulty with receiving good things in your life? Finding patterns is like mining for gold.

Identify the limiting beliefs

Sometimes simply identifying the old ideas and core beliefs that have been holding you back is enough to make the shift you need. If you've been carrying around a story since you were five years old and you finally realise that this has been affecting your behaviour for years, it can be incredibly liberating to finally recognise it and let it go. Other times, you may need to come up with new, affirming ideas and beliefs that challenge your existing ones. Look for evidence that your old ideas aren't necessarily true and that supports a new, more empowering view of yourself and what's possible for you.

Practice makes permanent

When it comes to changing your beliefs, thinking only takes you so far. What you need is direct, lived experience that supports your new ideas and perceptions. In psychology, we use behavioural experiments to challenge fearful thinking and gather evidence to support a different idea or world view. The more direct evidence you have that an idea is true, the more it becomes a belief and even a firm conviction. Essentially, you want to come up with a new idea about what's possible for you and then work out how you'd behave if that was really true for you. *Then do that.* Sometimes, you might benefit from the help of a coach or therapist to uncover the self-defeating thinking that's undermining your success. Meanwhile, remember the famous quote by Marianne Williamson: 'It is our light, not our darkness that most frightens us.'

Step nine

EXPECT GOOD THINGS

Do you consider yourself to be a glass-half-empty or a glass-half-full kind of person?

As part of your natural disposition, you no doubt tend towards being either optimistic (ever hopeful of a good outcome) or pessimistic (always erring on the side of caution). Sometimes, a little bit of pessimism is what's required in a situation, because optimists tend to exaggerate hopeful possibilities and minimise or downplay risk. Many occupations that require cautious scepticism or a focus on finding error or fault are well suited to people who naturally take a more pessimistic approach to things.

Having said that, there is no denying that optimistic people tend to be happier. According to research, they are more successful at work, earn more money and get promoted more often. They are more likely to be married and have happier relationships. Optimistic salespeople earn more money in commissions. Optimists enjoy better health and even live longer. So even if optimism doesn't come completely naturally to you, there is a whole lot to be gained by learning to apply a little more rose colour to your glasses.

> "Even if optimism doesn't come completely naturally to you, there is a whole lot to be gained by learning to apply a little more rose colour to your glasses."

WHEN OPTIMISM FEELS SCARY

In some cases, you might have started out expecting good things, only to have life beat the optimism out of you. If you've experienced a lot of adversity or challenge or had the rug pulled out from under you just when things were going well, it can seem like a safer option to stop expecting good outcomes in order to avoid disappointment. Perhaps feeling happy makes you feel especially vulnerable, because that's when it feels like you've got the most to lose. Rather than savouring the joy you might be experiencing in the present, you anxiously wait for the other shoe to drop. The rationale for that kind of thinking is that if you don't let yourself feel too happy, you won't be disappointed, because you've 'prepared yourself' for the worst.

It's important we do a reality check on that kind of thinking. If the worst-case scenario does indeed happen, it will be no less painful for you, regardless of how well you think you have prepared yourself. Refusing to allow yourself to feel joy in order to steel yourself against the possibility of pain means you're denying yourself the happiness that is here for the taking right now. Back in Step 3 we talked about the fact that none of us likes to experience painful emotions and we come up with all kinds of clever strategies to avoid discomfort. But as we already discussed, many of those strategies create even more problems in the long term.

Maybe it feels like you've already had your fair share of painful experiences and you can't deal with any more. Here's the thing, though ... if life is going to continue to throw you curve balls (and that's a big IF – there's just as much chance it will hand you success and happiness), the only possible way to shift the balance is to absorb and appreciate as much of the good stuff as you can get for as long as it chooses to show up in your life. That's the only way to increase the ratio of positive to negative emotions. The alternative is to feel crappy when things are crappy and then refuse to let yourself feel happy when things are going well; in other words, to keep feeling crappy *just in case* the happiness doesn't last. It doesn't make sense.

You deserve to live
a rich, fulfilling,
meaningful life.
Expect nothing less.

YOU'LL FIND WHAT YOU'RE LOOKING FOR

One of the known benefits of being an optimist is that your brain has a way of searching out and finding evidence to support your existing ideas. That's called 'confirmation bias'. This means that when our brain is doing its job of filtering what comes into our field of conscious awareness, it prioritises things that support our existing ideas or beliefs. This holds for philosophical and political views, parenting styles and opinions on just about anything. Essentially, your brain is designed to keep you comfortable and avoid internal tension by making sure it finds the evidence that you're right, and dismissing, denying or minimising any information that contradicts your point of view.

When it comes to your mood, if you have the thought that it's going to be a bad day, your mind will very obediently go looking for evidence that you *are* having a bad day. It's not personal as far as your brain is concerned. It's just doing its job. This makes it easy to see how we can be our own worst enemy. If you tell yourself that everything is going to turn out badly, you are going to find the evidence of that, even if there is competing evidence that things are actually going to be okay. If you have a belief that your mother never listens to you or that your husband doesn't respect you, you will find the evidence that this is true every single time. When people behave in a way that contradicts your existing point of view, you'll likely not notice it, or you'll come up with a justification that supports your existing beliefs (e.g. she's just feeling guilty, or he's trying to manipulate me), or you'll write it off as a fluke.

On the other hand, if you expect it's going to be a good day, you're more likely to spot the evidence of that. If there is just as much likelihood that things will turn out well as that they won't, why not focus on the potential positive and alert your brain to find the evidence that it's a good day?

LEARNING OPTIMISM

Optimism is partly a personality trait or disposition. In the field of positive psychology, there is another definition of optimism. Professor Martin Seligman once proved a theory that when something goes badly for you, you will use either an optimistic or pessimistic way of explaining that event. For example, if you lose your job or fail an exam, we each have a tendency to explain that failure or disappointment in a way that is either hopeful of a better outcome in the future, or defeatist and not hopeful of things ever turning around. Using an optimistic explanation when things go wrong can help keep your spirits up and make you more resilient in the face of setbacks. The good news is that when you understand optimism as an explanatory style, you can actively work on developing a positive way of explaining negative events. This is called 'Learned Optimism'.

Seligman hypothesised that there are three components to how we explain things that go wrong, and they are the 'Three Ps': permanence, pervasiveness and personalisation. In a pessimistic explanation, this setback is permanent ('I'll never succeed'), it pervades all areas ('My whole life is ruined') and it is entirely personal ('It's all my fault').

In a more optimistic explanation, this setback is temporary ('I'll learn from this and try again later because there will always be other opportunities'), it is limited to a small part of your life ('It's only a job – I still have my friends and my health') and it is not entirely personal ('You never know who else was competing for the job – it just wasn't my day').

As you can see, a pessimistic explanation will leave you feeling hopeless and defeated, whereas an optimistic explanation allows for hopeful possibilities despite this setback. With a little self-awareness, you can start listening in to your own negative self-talk and catch some of those pessimistic explanations. It might not feel natural to you at first, especially if you have a longstanding pattern of assuming the worst, but with practice you can change your explanatory style to one that is more optimistic, and you too can reap the benefits of a more optimistic perspective.

Create a compelling
vision of your ideal
future and take action
every day to bring
it into reality.

VISUALISE SUCCESS

In coaching, we often ask clients to create a detailed image in their minds of what life will look like when they achieve their goals. We ask them to breathe as much life and emotion into this imagined 'ideal future' as possible. Where will they be? Who will they be with? How will they feel? Doing this exercise is not fantasy – it's a proven way of motivating people towards goals, clarifying their values and increasing their chances of achieving their aims.

Performing an action in your mind is also a psychological skill used by athletes that has been shown to improve performance. In fact, basketball players who imagined themselves shooting hoops have been found to achieve the same levels of improvement as athletes who physically practised. Mental rehearsal can also be used to imagine and practise doing any action, such as giving a presentation, having a difficult conversation or going on a date. The idea is that you don't watch yourself as if in a movie, but rather you put yourself into the first person and go through the motions in your mind, feeling calm and confident as you do. This kind of visual imagery improves both performance and wellbeing. If you are a person who normally anticipates things going badly, it's a great exercise to keep your mind focused on the possibility of things going well.

As if by magic

When you become very clear about what you want to create in your life and you visualise it coming to fruition, never doubting that it will happen, it often has a way of appearing. You don't have to suddenly start believing in magic, but there is some power in holding steadfastly to a vision of what is possible and then methodically moving towards it. Believing in a benevolent universe that supports you feels a whole lot better than believing the world is against you, and that you'll never achieve anything. If everything you imagine is simply that – *imagination* – why not start imagining a brilliant future instead of assuming that things will never turn out the way you want? There is nothing to lose and everything to gain by expecting that things will go your way.

HOW TO TURN THINGS AROUND

Notice good things

Make a choice in the morning to notice a minimum of three good things that happen each day. They only need to be small things. A pleasant chat with a work colleague, a run of green lights or a really good cup of coffee, for example. As we've already discussed, your brain has a way of scanning your environment and finding what you tell it to look for. After a few days you'll notice that your brain is more primed to see the good things. It might feel like there are suddenly more good things in your world when in fact, it's not the world that changes but your own perception and what you choose to focus on.

Paint a mental picture

Writing a detailed account of your 'ideal future' or 'your best self' is a positive psychology exercise proven to boost happiness and wellbeing. You can practise being more optimistic by visualising an ideal future and reminding yourself that a positive outcome is just as likely as a disappointing one. You can do this for a particular scenario, such as applying for a job or trying to get pregnant, or you can use it to imagine an ideal future for you.

Remember the three Ps

In the face of a setback, try to challenge pessimistic thinking that leaves you feeling hopeless. Use the three Ps of **personalisation**, **permanence** and **pervasiveness** to come up with a new, more optimistic explanation for a disappointing outcome.

Step ten

MAKE A
DIFFERENCE

I believe we all instinctively want to leave the world a better place or to know that in the time we were here, we made a positive difference.

Much of this book has focused on how to increase your ratio of positive emotions to negative ones. There's no doubt this will go a long way to making you happier, but ultimately it is having a sense of purpose and contributing to something greater than your own self-interest that gives your life meaning.

Many researchers and philosophers are convinced that we should spend less of our energy on the pursuit of happiness and more on finding meaning. As you know, I believe to truly flourish we must give attention to both.

Pursuing only the good times in life and having a desire to be shielded from adversity and challenge creates a life only half lived. The activities that are the most meaningful in life are often not the most pleasant. Avoiding pain and suffering means denying yourself the opportunity to find out how strong, capable and resilient you really are. What you do with your pain and how you use it as a catalyst for your own growth or to benefit others can determine whether that suffering is in vain or if it paves the way to meaning.

Of course, living a life of meaning doesn't mean having to suffer! We can derive a sense of meaning and purpose from the same activities that also give us joy if we're smart about who we spend our time with and where we invest our energy. Giving back to your local community, volunteering for a cause close to your heart or doing work that makes you feel you are making a contribution are all meaningful activities that can also bring you great pleasure. Knowing that you have had a positive effect on someone else's life can be the most meaningful thing of all.

OUR INSTINCT TO GIVE BACK

Psychologist Erik Erikson's theory of psychosocial human development (1959) posited that there are certain psychological tasks that every person must complete at each stage of life in order to develop in a healthy way. Each life stage involves a crisis or a conflict between the needs of the individual and the needs of society. According to Erikson's model, between the ages of approximately forty and sixty-five, the developmental conflict to be resolved is the choice between whether to leave a legacy or to stagnate. He used the term 'generativity' to describe the developmental task of giving back – whether by raising children, mentoring a younger generation or contributing in some way to the community or the world. Many people with no knowledge of psychological theory would vouch that this is reflective of their personal experience.

In youth and even young adulthood, much of our energy is consumed with completing tasks we assume are expected of us. We go to school and then perhaps to university or begin a career. In adulthood, we begin making decisions about what we want from life. Will I get married? Have children? How important is career to me? Would I rather travel or pursue the arts or volunteer abroad? We are very much consumed with our own self-interest and our personal goals. We feel pressure to 'keep up' and achieve what we think society expects of us in a particular time frame.

There comes a time in life for all of us – and granted, I think for some people this happens sooner rather than later – where we begin to put aside our own objectives, personal motivations and other peoples' expectations and ask how we can make a difference to the world around us. As the saying goes, you can spend your life climbing a ladder only to reach the top and realise that the whole time, you had your ladder up against the wrong wall.

We begin to reflect on what we want our life to have been about. What is the legacy you will leave? How will you have made a difference, on either a small or a large scale? We realise that what's going to give our lives a sense of meaning and purpose is feeling that we have had a positive impact on other people's lives.

To truly flourish we
need to feel that our
life is in some way
meaningful.

FINDING YOUR PURPOSE

For many seekers of deep, lasting happiness, one of the great questions they ask of themselves is, 'What is my purpose? Why am I here on this earth?'

In the same way that the advice to 'follow your passion' can put pressure on people who aren't sure what they're passionate about, being told to 'find your purpose' can feel like an impossible burden. I think the problem is that we can easily buy into the idea that we have one true calling in life, which is much like the idea of the one true soulmate who will complete you. If you're under the impression that you are destined to have a single great purpose, something you were put on this earth to achieve, that suggests that if you don't find it, your life has been wasted.

For this reason, I don't necessarily subscribe to the notion that you must find your one true purpose. I do believe it's possible to have a primary mission that drives you; I just don't think it's essential for a fulfilling or meaningful life. I think feeling a sense of purpose in life involves living with intention, and making conscious choices every day about the impact you want to have. I think there are three important questions to be answered:

1. What are your strengths?

2. What matters most to you?

3. How can you be of service?

YOUR UNIQUE GIFTS

We all have our own unique qualities, traits and strengths. In psychology, the term 'strengths' refers to the things you are naturally good at and enjoy doing, and also describes the character traits that are most important to you. The problem for many people is that they either undervalue their own strengths or they simply don't recognise them. If something comes easily to you, you tend to take it for granted and not realise that this gift of yours is not something that everyone possesses.

Maybe you can walk into a room and immediately start redesigning it in your mind to maximise the light and space. You might be the social glue that holds a group of people together. You might have a knack for numbers or fashion or for reading people's faces. Again, you might not normally place any value on these things, but they're all clues about what makes you tick. This is really an exercise in understanding *who you are.* The more you apply your strengths in your life and work, the happier and more fulfilled you will be.

> **"If something comes easily to you, you tend to take it for granted and not realise that this gift of yours is not something that everyone possesses."**

The VIA Institute offers a free online assessment of an individual's character strengths. They have defined character strengths as a collection of twenty-four humanistic qualities that we all possess in varying degrees. These include qualities such as bravery, hope, persistence and gratitude. Having regular opportunities to use your character strengths in a meaningful way is one of the foundations of a flourishing life.

WHAT BREAKS YOUR HEART?

Dr Tererai Trent asked this question in a 2018 interview with Maria Shriver. The answer, which must come from your heart, not your mind, provides clues to your values, passion and purpose.

I remember scrolling through Facebook one day in January 2016 and coming across a live-streamed video of dolphins being slaughtered in Taiji Cove, Japan. My heart broke into a million pieces. I wanted to immediately pack my bags and head to Japan as a volunteer. That first impulse was highly impractical, but it reminded me of something I felt deeply passionate about, which is the welfare and protection of animals. Later I booked a trip to Borneo, where my ten-year-old daughter and I volunteered on a wildlife conservation project, helping to ensure the future of orangutans. I was able to contribute to a cause dear to my heart while also sharing the experience with my child, and hopefully teaching her the value of service and contribution.

Perhaps what breaks your heart is the plight of refugees, the ill-treatment of women and girls or the lack of funding for the homeless. Perhaps it is climate change, bullying in schools, youth mental health or cancer. It might be all of those things. But living a life with passion and purpose begins with finding ways to contribute to a cause that means something to you.

> "Living a life with passion and purpose begins with finding ways to contribute to a cause that means something to you."

DO WHAT YOU LOVE

Sometimes the most important thing is to let go of the idea of making your mark on the world on a grand scale, and instead find small ways to express your unique gifts. It is the greatest waste of a person's potential and a recipe for misery to have talents that are not being expressed in any meaningful way.

If you love to write, then write. If you tell yourself that your writing is meaningless unless it's reaching thousands of people or earning you a book deal, you're wasting your gift. If you have a flair for colour and style, start helping your friends with their home decoration or personal styling. Notice how it feels to do what comes most naturally to you in ways that have a positive impact on the people around you. The difference you make has a ripple effect out into the world. With your daily choice of actions and the energy you project, you either make people's days a little bit brighter and lighter, or you add to their troubles with your own.

HOW CAN I CONTRIBUTE?

A funny thing happens when you ask yourself this question. Your own ego and personal agenda are forced to take a back seat as you direct your attention outwards, to the people and world around you. You become less concerned about success or failure when you are focused on being of value. In our fast-paced, highly competitive and hyper-connected world, often it's the little things that make the biggest difference. It might be pausing long enough to ask someone how their week is going, and then really listening to the response. Noticing and complimenting someone on their haircut or outfit costs nothing, but it brightens the other person's day.

Choosing to cooperate instead of compete can be an unexpected and welcome gesture of goodwill in our 'dog eat dog' world. It's simply a matter of stepping out of our own self-absorbed preoccupations and wondering, just for a moment, about someone else's experience. It's having the thought that you could make a difference to someone and then acting on it.

Instead of rushing through life being consumed by your own worries and problems, it's looking outwards and offering compassion to others.

When you reach the end of your life, you want to know that you made a difference. Whether in big ways or small ways, we all need to know that our life had meaning and this, ultimately, will be our greatest satisfaction and joy.

"Whether in big ways or small ways, we all need to know that our life had meaning and this, ultimately, will be our greatest satisfaction and joy."

LIVING ON PURPOSE

Uncover your strengths

If you're unsure where your strengths lie, you might take an online assessment such as VIA Strengths or the Clifton Strengths Finder. Another useful exercise, if you're comfortable enough to do it, is to survey your friends and family about what they perceive to be your unique talents, gifts or character traits. Other people's perceptions of you can highlight strengths you may have been taking for granted. Look for opportunities to use your strengths.

Know what matters

Spend time reflecting on what matters most to you and the legacy you want to leave. Coaches will sometimes ask people to write their own obituary. It's a confronting exercise, but one that directly connects you to what you want your life to stand for and how you would like to be remembered. If you are able to hold that in mind when making decisions, it can serve as a North Star, guiding you towards your most meaningful, purpose-driven life.

Be of service

As you begin each day, ask yourself the question, 'How can I contribute?' This is not about subjugating your own needs in favour of others' demands, but about directing your attention to the ways you can add value to a person, an organisation or a cause that is greater than your own self-interest. Focusing on contribution gives new meaning to the tasks and activities that you perform every day. If you must do things that you don't find enjoyable, make the task meaningful by reflecting on how your involvement is making a difference.

As Pastor Rob Bell says in his book *How to Be Here*, 'You are a unique phenomenon in the history of the universe.' There has never been another one of you, and there never will be again. Live your life as if it matters, and as if what you do makes a difference, because every day, in big and small ways, it really does.

Acknowledgements

This book is the result of many years spent learning from wise teachers and mentors.

A few have been particularly significant in helping me become the best psychologist, coach and meditation teacher I can be. Dr Michael Cavanagh and Professor Tony Grant founded the Masters of Coaching Psychology, which kicked off my coaching career. I'm so grateful to have learned from two of the true greats in this industry. Dr Suzy Green taught the positive psychology subject in that program and was a breath of fresh air to me, the lone life coach in a room full of exec coaches, wondering if I had any place there. I'm grateful to now call Suzy a friend and colleague.

When I undertook my clinical psychology training, Dr Maura Kenny and Dr Ros Powrie became wise and warm mentors and role models. Both brilliant psychiatrists and teachers, they also helped me understand that being a mental health professional and being a flawed and imperfect person are not mutually exclusive; in fact, our shared struggles can be our greatest strengths.

This book may not have come about so quickly if not for the outstanding success of the *Crappy to Happy* podcast. I have to thank my friend and co-host Tiffiny Hall and our amazing producer, Dave Zwolenski, for making our show so fabulous.

The team at Hardie Grant publishing has been fantastic to work with, and I'm grateful to Pam and Emily for helping bring this book to life.

My greatest debt of gratitude has to be to my husband, Mel Dunn, for his years of unwavering support. He has encouraged me to pursue my passions, seen me launch various businesses, supported me financially when I went back to university (three times!) and held the fort at home while I disappeared on meditation retreats and writing sabbaticals. It's fair to say that none of this would be possible without him.

To my friends, family, clients, colleagues, podcast listeners and online community – my deep gratitude for your ongoing support. I learn as much from you all as I hope you do from me.

Published in 2019 by Hardie Grant Books,
an imprint of Hardie Grant Publishing

Hardie Grant Books (Melbourne)
Building 1, 658 Church Street
Richmond, Victoria 3121

Hardie Grant Books (London)
5th & 6th Floors
52–54 Southwark Street
London SE1 1UN

hardiegrantbooks.com

A catalogue record for this
book is available from the
National Library of Australia

Crappy to Happy: Simple Steps to Live Your Best Life
ISBN 978 1 74379 511 8

10 9 8 7 6 5 4 3 2 1

Cover and text design by Alissa Dinallo
Typeset in Gotham Book by Kirby Jones

Colour reproduction by Splitting Image Colour Studio
Printed in China by Leo Paper Product. LTD